This diving log belongs to:

_____

_____

_____

_____

*The best way to observe a fish is to become
a fish.*

-Jacques Cousteau

certifications

course

date completed

instructor & number

location

notes

course

date completed

instructor & number

location

notes

course

date completed

instructor & number

location

notes

course

date completed

instructor & number

location

notes

certifications

course

date completed

instructor & number

location

notes

---

course

date completed

instructor & number

location

notes

---

course

date completed

instructor & number

location

notes

---

course

date completed

instructor & number

location

notes

dive no.

dive stats

air in	suit	weight	air out	total dive time

time in	safety stop	time out	
O₂%	visibility	air temp	notes
max depth	bottom time	water temp	

my dive experience

weather	surface conditions	type of dive

stamp & authentication

dive no.

name of dive site   date

location

dive stats

| air in | suit | weight | air out | total dive time |

time in	safety stop	time out	
O₂%	visibility	air temp	notes
max depth	bottom time	water temp	

my dive experience

| weather | surface conditions | type of dive |

stamp & authentication

dive no.

name of dive site   date

location

dive stats

air in	suit	weight	air out	total dive time

time in	safety stop	time out
O₂%	visibility	air temp
max depth	bottom time	water temp

notes

my dive experience

weather   surface conditions   type of dive

stamp & authentication

dive no.

name of dive site   date

location

dive stats

| air in | suit | weight | air out | total dive time |

time in	safety stop	time out	
O₂%	visibility	air temp	
max depth	bottom time	water temp	notes

my dive experience

weather   surface conditions   type of dive

stamp & authentication

dive no.

name of dive site

date

location

dive stats

air in

suit

weight

air out

total dive time

time in

safety stop

time out

O_2%

visibility

air temp

max depth

bottom time

water temp

notes

my dive experience

weather

surface conditions

type of dive

stamp & authentication

dive no.

name of dive site _____ date

location _____

dive stats

| air in | suit | weight | air out | total dive time |

time in	safety stop	time out	
O₂%	visibility	air temp	notes
max depth	bottom time	water temp	

my dive experience

| weather | surface conditions | type of dive |

stamp & authentication

dive no.

name of dive site

date

location

dive stats

| air in | suit | weight | air out | total dive time |

time in	safety stop	time out
O₂%	visibility	air temp
max depth	bottom time	water temp

notes

my dive experience

weather | surface conditions | type of dive

stamp & authentication

dive no.

name of dive site   date

location

dive stats

air in | suit | weight | air out | total dive time

time in | safety stop | time out

O₂% | visibility | air temp

max depth | bottom time | water temp

notes

my dive experience

weather | surface conditions | type of dive

stamp & authentication

dive no.

name of dive site   date

location

dive stats

air in	suit	weight	air out	total dive time

time in	safety stop	time out	
O₂%	visibility	air temp	
max depth	bottom time	water temp	notes

my dive experience

weather	surface conditions	type of dive

stamp & authentication

dive no.

name of dive site   date

location

dive stats

| air in | suit | weight | air out | total dive time |

| time in | safety stop | time out |

| O₂% | visibility | air temp |

| max depth | bottom time | water temp |

notes

my dive experience

weather   surface conditions   type of dive

stamp & authentication

dive no.

name of dive site   date

location

dive stats

air in | suit | weight | air out | total dive time

time in | safety stop | time out

O₂% | visibility | air temp

max depth | bottom time | water temp

notes

my dive experience

weather | surface conditions | type of dive

stamp & authentication

dive no.

name of dive site   date

location

dive stats

air in	suit	weight	air out	total dive time

time in	safety stop	time out	
O₂%	visibility	air temp	notes
max depth	bottom time	water temp	

my dive experience

weather   surface conditions   type of dive

stamp & authentication

dive no.

dive stats

air in	suit	weight	air out	total dive time

time in	safety stop	time out	
O₂%	visibility	air temp	notes
max depth	bottom time	water temp	

my dive experience

weather	surface conditions	type of dive

stamp & authentication

dive no.

dive stats

| air in | suit | weight | air out | total dive time |

time in	safety stop	time out
O₂%	visibility	air temp
max depth	bottom time	water temp

notes

my dive experience

| weather | surface conditions | type of dive |

stamp & authentication

dive no.

name of dive site   date

location

dive stats

air in | suit | weight | air out | total dive time

time in | safety stop | time out

O₂% | visibility | air temp

max depth | bottom time | water temp

notes

my dive experience

weather | surface conditions | type of dive

stamp & authentication

dive no.

location

dive stats

air in	suit	weight	air out	total dive time

time in	safety stop	time out	
O₂%	visibility	air temp	
max depth	bottom time	water temp	notes

my dive experience

weather	surface conditions	type of dive

stamp & authentication

dive no.

name of dive site   date

location

dive stats

air in   suit   weight   air out   total dive time

time in   safety stop   time out

O₂%   visibility   air temp

max depth   bottom time   water temp

notes

my dive experience

weather   surface conditions   type of dive

stamp & authentication

dive no.

name of dive site   date

location

dive stats

air in	suit	weight	air out	total dive time

time in	safety stop	time out	notes
O2%	visibility	air temp	
max depth	bottom time	water temp	

my dive experience

weather	surface conditions	type of dive

stamp & authentication

dive no.

name of dive site   date

location

dive stats

air in | suit | weight | air out | total dive time

time in | safety stop | time out

O₂% | visibility | air temp

max depth | bottom time | water temp

notes

my dive experience

weather | surface conditions | type of dive

stamp & authentication

dive no.

name of dive site   date

location

dive stats

| air in | suit | weight | air out | total dive time |

time in	safety stop	time out	
O₂%	visibility	air temp	
max depth	bottom time	water temp	notes

my dive experience

| weather | surface conditions | type of dive |

stamp & authentication

dive no.

name of dive site   date

location

dive stats

air in	suit	weight	air out	total dive time

time in	safety stop	time out	
O₂%	visibility	air temp	notes
max depth	bottom time	water temp	

my dive experience

weather	surface conditions	type of dive

stamp & authentication

dive no.

name of dive site   date

location

dive stats

air in	suit	weight	air out	total dive time

time in	safety stop	time out	
O₂%	visibility	air temp	
max depth	bottom time	water temp	notes

my dive experience

weather	surface conditions	type of dive

stamp & authentication

dive no.

name of dive site   date

location

dive stats

| air in | suit | weight | air out | total dive time |

time in	safety stop	time out	
O₂%	visibility	air temp	
max depth	bottom time	water temp	notes

my dive experience

weather   surface conditions   type of dive

stamp & authentication

dive no.

location

dive stats

| air in | suit | weight | air out | total dive time |

time in	safety stop	time out	
O₂%	visibility	air temp	
max depth	bottom time	water temp	

notes

my dive experience

| weather | surface conditions | type of dive |

stamp & authentication

dive no.

name of dive site   date

location

dive stats

air in | suit | weight | air out | total dive time

time in | safety stop | time out

O_2% | visibility | air temp

max depth | bottom time | water temp

notes

my dive experience

weather | surface conditions | type of dive

stamp & authentication

dive no.

name of dive site   date

location

dive stats

air in	suit	weight	air out	total dive time

time in	safety stop	time out	
O₂%	visibility	air temp	notes
max depth	bottom time	water temp	

my dive experience

weather	surface conditions	type of dive

stamp & authentication

dive no.

name of dive site   date

location

dive stats

| air in | suit | weight | air out | total dive time |

| time in | safety stop | time out | |

| O₂% | visibility | air temp | |

| max depth | bottom time | water temp | notes |

my dive experience

| weather | surface conditions | type of dive |

stamp & authentication

dive no.

name of dive site date

location

dive stats

air in	suit	weight	air out	total dive time

time in	safety stop	time out	

O₂%	visibility	air temp	notes

max depth	bottom time	water temp	

my dive experience

weather	surface conditions	type of dive

stamp & authentication

dive no.

name of dive site   date

location

dive stats

| air in | suit | weight | air out | total dive time |

time in | safety stop | time out

O₂% | visibility | air temp

max depth | bottom time | water temp

notes

my dive experience

weather | surface conditions | type of dive

stamp & authentication

dive no.

name of dive site

date

location

dive stats

air in | suit | weight | air out | total dive time

time in | safety stop | time out

O₂% | visibility | air temp

max depth | bottom time | water temp

notes

my dive experience

weather | surface conditions | type of dive

stamp & authentication

dive no.

name of dive site

date

location

dive stats

air in

suit

weight

air out

total dive time

time in

safety stop

time out

O₂%

visibility

air temp

max depth

bottom time

water temp

notes

my dive experience

weather

surface conditions

type of dive

stamp & authentication

dive no.

name of dive site _____ date

location

dive stats

| air in | suit | weight | air out | total dive time |

time in	safety stop	time out	
O₂%	visibility	air temp	notes
max depth	bottom time	water temp	

my dive experience

| weather | surface conditions | type of dive |

stamp & authentication

dive no.

name of dive site | date

location

dive stats

air in | suit | weight | air out | total dive time

time in | safety stop | time out

O₂% | visibility | air temp

max depth | bottom time | water temp

notes

my dive experience

weather | surface conditions | type of dive

stamp & authentication

dive no.

name of dive site   date

location

dive stats

air in | suit | weight | air out | total dive time

time in | safety stop | time out

O₂% | visibility | air temp

max depth | bottom time | water temp

notes

my dive experience

weather | surface conditions | type of dive

stamp & authentication

dive no.

name of dive site   date

location

dive stats

air in | suit | weight | air out | total dive time

time in | safety stop | time out

O₂% | visibility | air temp

max depth | bottom time | water temp

notes

my dive experience

weather | surface conditions | type of dive

stamp & authentication

dive no.

name of dive site   date

location

dive stats

air in	suit	weight	air out	total dive time

time in	safety stop	time out	
O₂%	visibility	air temp	notes
max depth	bottom time	water temp	

my dive experience

weather	surface conditions	type of dive

stamp & authentication

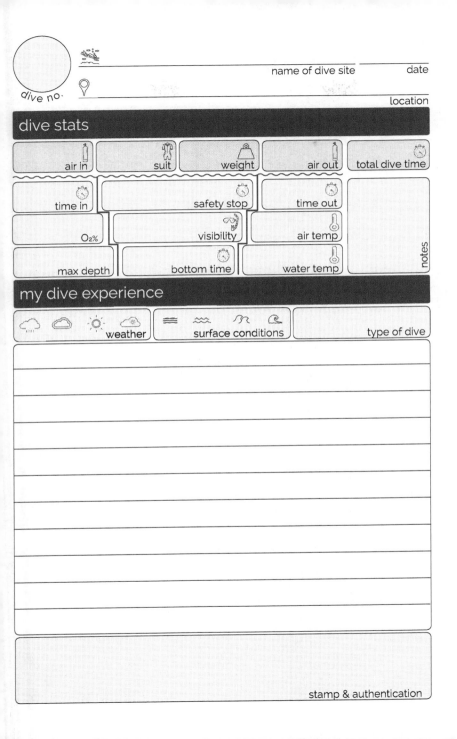

dive no.

name of dive site　　　　date

location

dive stats

air in　　suit　　weight　　air out　　total dive time

time in　　safety stop　　time out

O_2%　　visibility　　air temp

max depth　　bottom time　　water temp

notes

my dive experience

weather　　surface conditions　　type of dive

stamp & authentication

dive no.

name of dive site   date

location

dive stats

| air in | suit | weight | air out | total dive time |

time in	safety stop	time out
O_2%	visibility	air temp
max depth	bottom time	water temp

notes

my dive experience

weather   surface conditions   type of dive

stamp & authentication

dive no.

name of dive site   date

location

dive stats

air in | suit | weight | air out | total dive time

time in | safety stop | time out

O₂% | visibility | air temp

max depth | bottom time | water temp

notes

my dive experience

weather | surface conditions | type of dive

stamp & authentication

dive no.

name of dive site   date

location

dive stats

air in | suit | weight | air out | total dive time

time in | safety stop | time out

O₂% | visibility | air temp

max depth | bottom time | water temp

notes

my dive experience

weather | surface conditions | type of dive

stamp & authentication

dive no.

name of dive site

date

location

dive stats

air in | suit | weight | air out | total dive time

time in | safety stop | time out

O₂% | visibility | air temp

max depth | bottom time | water temp

notes

my dive experience

weather | surface conditions | type of dive

stamp & authentication

dive no.

name of dive site   date

location

dive stats

air in | suit | weight | air out | total dive time

time in | safety stop | time out

O₂% | visibility | air temp

max depth | bottom time | water temp

notes

my dive experience

weather | surface conditions | type of dive

stamp & authentication

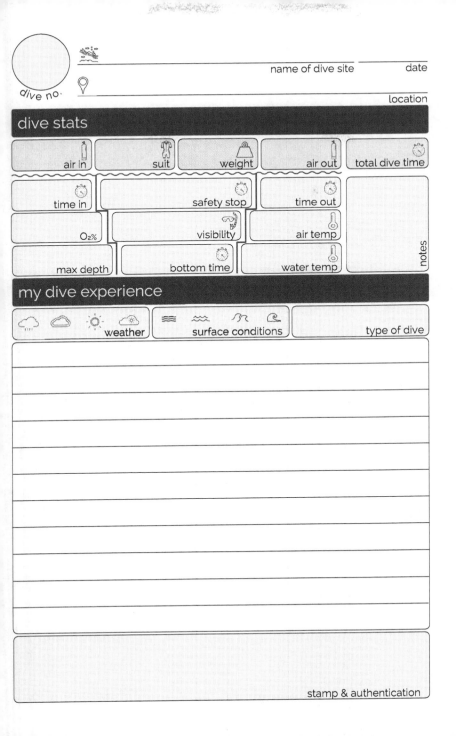

dive no.

name of dive site   date

location

dive stats

air in | suit | weight | air out | total dive time

time in

safety stop

time out

O₂%

visibility

air temp

max depth

bottom time

water temp

notes

my dive experience

weather | surface conditions | type of dive

stamp & authentication

dive no.

dive stats

air in	suit	weight	air out	total dive time

time in	safety stop	time out	
O₂%	visibility	air temp	notes
max depth	bottom time	water temp	

my dive experience

weather	surface conditions	type of dive

stamp & authentication

dive no.

name of dive site

date

location

dive stats

air in | suit | weight | air out | total dive time

time in | safety stop | time out

O₂% | visibility | air temp

max depth | bottom time | water temp

notes

my dive experience

weather | surface conditions | type of dive

stamp & authentication

dive no.

name of dive site   date

location

dive stats

air in | suit | weight | air out | total dive time

time in | safety stop | time out

O₂% | visibility | air temp

max depth | bottom time | water temp

notes

my dive experience

weather | surface conditions | type of dive

stamp & authentication

dive no.

name of dive site   date

location

dive stats

| air in | suit | weight | air out | total dive time |

time in	safety stop	time out	
O₂%	visibility	air temp	notes
max depth	bottom time	water temp	

my dive experience

| weather | surface conditions | type of dive |

stamp & authentication

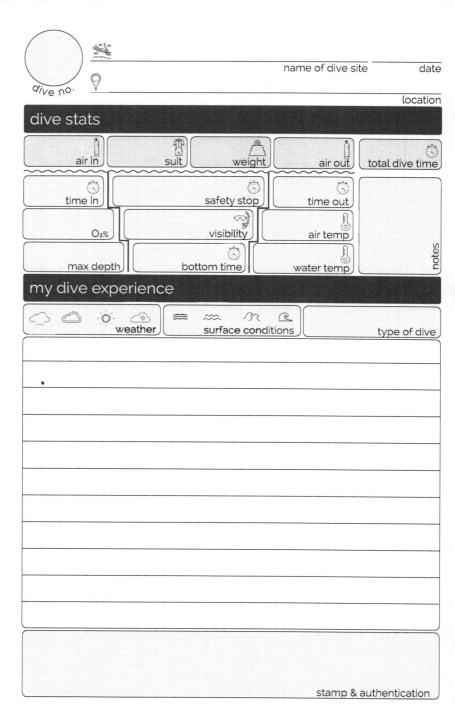

dive no.

name of dive site   date

location

dive stats

air in   suit   weight   air out   total dive time

time in   safety stop   time out

O₂%   visibility   air temp

max depth   bottom time   water temp

notes

my dive experience

weather   surface conditions   type of dive

•

stamp & authentication

dive no.

name of dive site   date

location

dive stats

air in | suit | weight | air out | total dive time

time in | safety stop | time out

O₂% | visibility | air temp

max depth | bottom time | water temp

notes

my dive experience

weather | surface conditions | type of dive

stamp & authentication

Made in the USA
Las Vegas, NV
27 May 2021

23740142R00035